UP DATE

The New Blueprint for Dating, Covenant
&
Becoming the One. *(Vol 1)*

By: Latia Ashley

ACKNOWLEDGMENTS

To God, who has been my foundation, my strength, and my guide thank You for Your grace, wisdom, and the unshakable love that has sustained me through every season. This book is a testament to Your faithfulness.

To my trusted pastors, who have poured into me with wisdom, encouragement, and unwavering support I honor and appreciate your dedication to shepherding hearts and helping me grow in purpose.

To my dear family & friends thank you for trusting me as a safe space, for sharing your journeys with me, and for allowing your wisdom and experiences to create speed bumps that slowed me down when I needed it most. Your honesty, laughter, and insights have shaped so much of this book.

May this book be a reflection of God's love, grace, and truth.

UPDATE

Table Of Contents

Why This Book?

Because dating is confusing, and nobody handed us a real guide. We've read books, heard sermons, and gotten advice from people who mean well but don't always know what they're talking about.

And let's be real sometimes, we've been the problem, too.

This book isn't just for singles trying to figure out relationships. It's for those who are married and can look back and say, *"I wish I had known this before,"* and could be for those who want to strengthen their marriage by revisiting the foundation of love, wisdom, and commitment. Because relationships don't start at the altar they start long before, in the way we prepare, heal, and choose.

Some of us have settled for breadcrumbs when we deserved the whole meal. Some of us have mistaken chemistry for covenant and learned the hard way that attraction alone won't keep a relationship together.

I wrote this book because I know what it feels like to be at a crossroads to want love but not want to lose yourself in the process. To wonder if your standards are too high or if you're just surrounded by people who can't meet them. To ask yourself if God is telling you to wait, or if He's telling you to walk away.

So, if you're tired of recycled advice that sounds good but doesn't actually help, you're in the right place.

This book isn't here to pressure you into a relationship, rush your process, or make you feel like something's wrong with you if you're single. It's here to help you move wisely, love intentionally, and break cycles that have kept you stuck.

Introduction: Let's Be Real for a Second

Can we really to talk about it?

Not even the Bible tells us exactly how to "date." It lays out wisdom for marriage, the qualities of a godly spouse, and the beauty of covenant but it doesn't hand us a step-by-step guide for navigating love in a world where ghosting, breadcrumbing, and commitment-phobia exist. And let's be honest figuring it out on our own hasn't exactly been working.

I don't know about you, but I've seen too many people fumble relationships not because they didn't love each other, but because they weren't ready for the weight of what love actually requires.

We've been sold a dream that love is just about finding the right person. But what if love is about becoming the right person first?

- **We say we want commitment, but are we prepared for it?**
- **We want a love that lasts, but do we know how to sustain it?**
- **We pray for a godly relationship, but are we truly healed enough to handle one?**

We don't just inherit a person in a relationship. We inherit their habits, their traumas, their family, and their unfinished business. That's why we need wisdom before emotions, purpose before passion, and healing before commitment. And that's what this book is about.

Chapter 1: The Myth of Completion

The Lie We've Been Sold

Since childhood, most of us have been fed a romanticized narrative about love: *Find the right person, and everything in your life will fall into place.* From Disney movies to rom coms, the message has been clear true love will complete you. Then you'll suddenly be happy, fulfilled, and whole.

But let's pause and be real: That's a lie.

A relationship does not magically fix your insecurities, heal your past trauma, or give you purpose. If anything, it magnifies whatever is already inside of you. If you feel unworthy while single, you'll still feel unworthy in a relationship. If you lack direction now, a spouse won't give you one. *Only God can do that.*

Colossians 2:10 (NLT):

"So you also are complete through your union with Christ, who is the head over every ruler and authority."

Your wholeness comes from God, not a partner. That means you are already enough as you are, and any relationships you enter should be about what you can give, not just what you can receive.

Broken People Create Broken Relationships

Picture this: You buy a beautiful glass vase, but it has a tiny crack in it. You ignore it, thinking it's nothing serious. Over time, water starts leaking out. Eventually, the crack deepens, and one day it shatters.

That's how unhealed emotional wounds work in relationships. If you enter a relationship thinking it will fix your loneliness, insecurities, or past heartbreaks, you're setting yourself up for disappointment and destruction.

Unhealed people don't just break relationships they sabotage them. They project past pain onto new partners, mistake attention for love, and expect another person to do what only God can do: make them whole.

If you don't deal with your emotional wounds now, they will follow you into every relationship you have. Healing isn't just nice before dating it's mandatory.

Psalm 147:3 (NLT):

"He heals the brokenhearted and bandages their wounds."

The good news? Healing is available to you. But it requires intentionality, self-reflection, and allowing God to do the deep work in your heart before you invite someone else into it.

-Friendships Are the Blueprint for Covenant Partnerships

One of the most overlooked truths about dating is this: Your friendships reveal how you will handle a romantic relationship.

Think about it—how do you treat your closest friends?

- Do you show up for them, or only when it's convenient?

- Do you communicate well, or do you ghost people when things get hard?

- Do you handle conflict with grace, or do you cut people off?

Proverbs 17:17 (NLT):

"A friend is always loyal, and a brother is born to help in time of need."

Marriage is not just romance it's friendship on the highest level. If you struggle to maintain healthy, godly friendships, you will struggle to build a strong marriage. The same principles that make friendships thrive loyalty, honesty, forgiveness, and selflessness are foundational for a covenant relationship.

Want to prepare for marriage? Start by being a better friend.

Healing Before Love: Addressing Heartbreak and Unforgiveness

Let's talk about heartbreak. Whether it's from a failed relationship, a broken friendship, or even wounds from your parents, unforgiveness will hold you hostage.

If you carry bitterness from your past, it will leak into your future. You'll find yourself doubting good people because of what someone toxic did to you. You'll sabotage potential relationships because you're still *waiting for an apology* from someone who will never give it.

Ephesians 4:31-32 (NLT):

"Get rid of all bitterness, rage, anger, harsh words, and slander, as well as all types of evil behavior. Instead, be kind to each other, tenderhearted, forgiving one another, just as God through Christ has forgiven you."

Forgiveness isn't about letting someone off the hook—it's about setting yourself free. You can't step into a healthy relationship if you're still dragging the baggage of past pain. Let it go. Not for them for you.

The Power of Intentional Singleness

Before you even think about dating, ask yourself: Have I truly taken the time to know myself?

Being intentionally single is not about waiting for "the one"—it's about using this season to grow, heal, and align with your purpose.

- What are your personal goals outside of relationships?

- Do you have a strong sense of identity, or are you looking for someone to define you?

- Are you comfortable being alone, or do you jump from relationship to relationship?

This time of singleness is a **gift** an opportunity to build the foundation of the life you want. The stronger your foundation, the healthier your future relationship will be. We will tackle more of this in a later chapter.

Heart Truth: You don't need another relationship to validate you. You don't need a partner to make you whole. If you're looking for love to fix you, you're looking for the wrong thing.

The truth is, love is not a magic cure it's a mirror. It will reveal what's inside of you, whether you like it or not. If you're still struggling with insecurities, trust issues, or unhealed wounds, those things won't disappear in a relationship they'll only get louder.

So, before you chase love, chase healing. Before you seek a partner, seek wholeness. Because when you show up complete, you don't need someone to fill a void you bring value to the table.

A Real-Life Moment

Out of respect I will leave names out but, I have been granted permission to share this story. I once knew someone who jumped from relationship to relationship, never staying single long enough to truly heal. For some reason, she believed that as long as she had someone by her side, she wouldn't have to face the pain of her past. But every relationship ended the same way broken, bitter, and blaming the other person for what she refused to confront within herself.

One day, after yet another breakup, she finally hit a breaking point. She sat in her car and cried, not just over the guy, but over the years of carrying wounds she never dealt with. It was in that moment she realized: *No relationship was ever going to fix what was broken inside of her.* She had to stop running from healing and start embracing the process of becoming whole.

That was the turning point. She took a break from dating, sought wise counsel, dove deeper into her faith, and let God mend what she kept covering up with relationships. And when she finally did enter a relationship again it wasn't out of need, but out of overflow.

Healing is a choice. And it's the best one you'll ever make.

Closing Thoughts

Wholeness isn't a destination it's a journey. God never intended for marriage to be a crutch for brokenness. Instead, He calls us to seek Him first, allowing Him to make us whole before we pursue love. When you step into a relationship already complete, you're not looking for someone to save you, you're looking for someone to build with. And that's the kind of love God desires for you.

Chapter 2: Covenant More Than a Contract

What Is a Covenant?

A covenant is a sacred, binding agreement between two parties that is based on trust, commitment, and sacrifice. Unlike a contract, which is built on terms and conditions that can be voided, a covenant is designed to be permanent and unbreakable.

Think of a Mafia blood oath once you're in, there's no backing out. This kind of loyalty and commitment is rare in today's relationships, where people tend to leave when things get tough. But God designed love and marriage to be covenantal, not contractual.

Another example is the covenant of adoption when parents legally adopt a child, they commit to loving, providing for, and caring for that child as their own, regardless of what happens in the future. There's no backing out because it's a lifetime commitment. That's what God intends for relationships: a lasting promise, not a temporary deal.

Malachi 2:14 (NLT):

"You cry out, 'Why doesn't the Lord accept my worship?' I'll tell you why! Because the Lord witnessed the vows you and your wife made when you were young. But you have been unfaithful to her, though she remained your faithful partner, the wife of your marriage vows. "God takes covenant seriously. In biblical times, covenants were sealed with blood, symbolizing their permanence. A covenant isn't just about words it's about action, responsibility, and commitment.

The Difference Between a Contract and a Covenant

In today's world, relationships are often treated like contracts a set of conditions that, if broken, allow one party to walk away. A contract says, *"I'll stay as long as you make me happy."* But a covenant? A covenant says, *"I am committed to you, no matter what."*

Marriage, according to God's design, was never meant to be transactional it was always meant to be sacrificial. Unlike a contract that is based on mutual benefit, a covenant is built on unconditional commitment.

Covenant Requires Sacrifice

Let's be real relationships today are built around comfort, convenience, and personal gain. We swipe left if we're not interested, cut people off at the first sign of discomfort, and treat love as disposable.

But a godly relationship a covenant partnership requires sacrifice.

- Are you willing to love someone even when they don't meet your expectations?

- Are you prepared to serve, even when it's inconvenient?

- Are you committed to staying, even when the emotions fade?

Ephesians 5:25 (NLT):

"For husbands, this means love your wives, just as Christ loved the church. He gave up his life for her."

Marriage is a reflection of Christ's love for the Church. And how did Christ love? He sacrificed. He stayed. He forgave. If your idea of commitment is conditional, then you're thinking contractually, not "covenantally".

Why Many People Struggle with Covenant

The truth? We live in a culture that fears commitment. We want the benefits of love without the responsibility. But this often stems from past wounds, distrust, and a fear of getting hurt.

Here's what stops people from embracing covenant relationships:

1. **Fear of Abandonment:** If you've been let down before, you may struggle to believe someone will truly stay.

2. **Unrealistic Expectations:** Some people believe love should always be effortless and passion filled.

3. **Selfishness:** Covenant is about giving, but culture has trained us to ask, *"What's in it for me?"*

Psalm 37:5 (NLT):

"Commit everything you do to the Lord. Trust him, and he will help you."

If you fear commitment, God wants to help heal your heart. He wants to replace fear with trust, selfishness with servanthood, and temporary thinking with eternal vision.

-Practical Exercises

1. **Covenant vs. Contract Check:** Make a list of how you currently approach relationships. Are your expectations contractual (only giving when it benefits you) or covenantal (committed even when it's hard)?

2. **Evaluate Your Friendships:** How do you handle conflict? Are you a loyal friend, or do you withdraw when things get tough?

3. **Prayer for Covenant Mindset:** Ask God to reveal areas where you need to grow in commitment, sacrifice, and unconditional love.

Journal Reflection

- Have I viewed relationships as contracts instead of covenants?

- What fears do I have about long-term commitment, and where do they come from?

- How can I practice sacrificial love in my friendships and relationships?

Closing Thoughts

Covenant love is not about what you can get it's about what you can give. True love mirrors Christ's sacrifice and commitment to His people. If you want to build a strong, lasting relationship, you must embrace the mindset of covenant over contract.

When you commit to loving beyond convenience, beyond comfort, beyond personal gain that's when you step into the kind of relationship God designed for you.

Covenant is costly, but real love always is.

Chapter 3: Dating in a Culture That Doesn't Value Commitment

The Shift in Modern Dating

Dating today looks vastly different from how it did just a few decades ago. With the rise of social media, dating apps, and a culture of instant gratification, many people now treat relationships as disposable. Commitment has become optional, and people often prioritize convenience over covenant.
In a world that encourages "talking stages," "situationships," and "ghosting," it's easy to feel lost.

But as a believer, your approach to dating should be radically different from the world's standards. The question is: ARE YOU DATING IN A WAY THAT HONORS GOD?

Romans 12:2 (NLT):
"Don't copy the behavior and customs of this world, but let God transform you into a new person by changing the way you think.

Then you will learn to know God's will for you, which is good and pleasing and perfect."

To date with purpose, you have to reject the culture's toxic norms and embrace a God centered mindset.

Why Commitment is Fading

People avoid commitment for many reasons:

- **Fear of Missing Out (FOMO):** Many believe that settling down means losing out on better options.

- **Fear of Vulnerability:** Deep connections require emotional risk, and many avoid that by keeping relationships casual.
- **Lack of Accountability:** Without strong faith and community, there's no pressure to honor commitments.

- **Unrealistic Expectations:** Social media highlights "perfect" relationships, leading people to chase illusions instead of building real connections.

Commitment is scary, but it's also the foundation of real love. If you are unwilling to commit, you are not ready to love.

The Hookup Culture vs. Covenant Dating

The world promotes a "hookup culture" where relationships are built on convenience, not commitment. But God calls you to something higher.

Comparison: Hookup Culture vs. Covenant Dating

Hookup Culture	Covenant Dating
Seeks pleasure	Seeks purpose
Avoids commitment	Embraces commitment
Instant gratification	Delayed gratification
Driven by emotion	Driven by wisdom
Temporary	Lifelong potential

If you approach dating with a **consumer mindset** always looking for the next best thing you will never build something that lasts. True love requires **intentionality.**

Think about it: The Fast-Food Relationship
Imagine you're starving, and you have two options:

1. A drive-thru meal that's fast, cheap, and instantly satisfying.
2. A home-cooked meal that takes time to prepare but is nutritious and fulfilling.

Most people choose the fast-food option it's easy, convenient, and doesn't require much effort. But over time, too much fast-food leads to health problems, regret, and dissatisfaction.

Dating works the same way. Many people opt for quick, shallow relationships that offer immediate pleasure but lack depth. But a God-centered relationship is like a home-cooked meal it requires patience, effort, and preparation, but the reward is lasting and fulfilling.

Which meal are you choosing?

How to Date with Intention

If you want a relationship that leads to marriage, you must date with purpose. That means:

- **Knowing Your Why:** Are you dating just to have fun, or are you seeking a partner for life?

- **Setting Standards:** Don't lower your values just to keep someone interested.

- **Guarding Your Heart:** Avoid emotional entanglements with people who don't align with your faith.

- **Seeking God First:** Your relationship with Christ should always be your first priority.

Proverbs 4:23 (NIV):
"Above all else, guard your heart, for everything you do flows from it." Intentional dating means honoring God, respecting yourself, and being clear about what you want.

Practical Exercises

1. **Self-Reflection:** Write down what you truly want in a relationship and compare it to what God desires for you.

2. **Social Media Detox:** Take a break from relationship comparisons on social media for one week and focus on your personal growth.

3. **Boundaries Check:** Identify areas where you've compromised your values in past relationships and set new, healthier boundaries.

Journal Reflection

- Am I dating in a way that honors God?

- Have I been influenced by the world's dating culture more than biblical principles?

- What steps can I take to date with greater intention and wisdom?

Closing Thoughts

Dating in today's culture can feel overwhelming, but you don't have to follow the world's broken system. You can choose a different path one that values commitment, honor, and faith.
By rejecting hookup culture and embracing covenant dating, you are setting the foundation for a God-glorifying relationship that will stand the test of time.

The question is, will you trust God's way, or will you settle for convenience?

Chapter 4: The Power of Intentional Singleness

Singleness is not a waiting room

For too long, singleness has been treated like a waiting season like an in between phase before REAL LIFE begins with a relationship. But singleness is not a punishment, and it is not something to rush through. It is a season of purpose, preparation, and identity.

Too many people enter relationships without ever truly knowing themselves. They don't take the time to develop emotional and spiritual maturity, and as a result, they expect another person to fulfill them in ways only God can. If you are not whole single, you will not be whole married.

Be Real Moment:
Singleness can be hard especially when it feels like everyone around you is in a relationship or starting a family. It's easy to feel like you're MISSING OUT or that you're somehow behind. But let's be honest: relationships don't cure loneliness. They don't erase insecurity. They don't automatically make you feel loved or fulfilled.

If you can't be content alone, you will never be content in a relationship. A partner should complement you, not complete you.

1 Corinthians 7:32-34 (NLT):

"I want you to be free from the concerns of this life. An unmarried man can spend his time doing the Lord's work and thinking how to please him. But a married man has to think about his earthly responsibilities and how to please his wife. His interests are divided. In the same way, a woman who is no longer married or has never been married can be devoted to the Lord and holy in body and in spirit. But a married woman has to think about her earthly responsibilities and how to please her husband."

Paul wasn't saying marriage is bad—he was saying that singleness is a unique season of undivided focus that should be used wisely.

What You Gain from Intentional Singleness

- **Clarity of Purpose:** When you are not distracted by relationship drama, you can clearly pursue your calling.

- **Spiritual Growth:** This is the time to develop your relationship with God without divided attention.

- **Emotional Maturity:** You learn how to regulate your emotions, handle conflict, and be secure in yourself.

- **Stronger Friendships:** You have time to invest in deep, meaningful friendships that will last a lifetime.

- **Freedom to Explore:** You can travel, try new things, and discover who you truly are without limitations.

Singleness is not about waiting**, it's about** becoming.

Think About It: The Person Who Rushed

I once knew someone who rushed into a relationship simply because they feared being alone. They felt pressured by family and social expectations, and instead of waiting for the right person, they settled for the next person available.

At first, everything seemed fine. But over time, it became clear they weren't actually compatible with their partner. They hadn't taken the time to develop emotional intelligence, set boundaries, or understand their personal values. Eventually, the relationship collapsed under the weight of unmet expectations.

Looking back, they admitted: "I spent so much time looking for love that I forgot to build a life I actually loved."
Rushing into a relationship out of fear of being alone can leave you feeling even lonelier inside of it.

Ecclesiastes 3:1 (NIV):
"There is a time for everything, and a season for every activity under the heavens."
Use this season well don't wish it away.

How to Be Intentional in Your Singleness

- **Focus on Your Purpose:** What has God called you to do in this season?

- **Heal & Grow:** Take time to work through past hurts and personal development.

- **Develop Healthy Relationships:** Build strong friendships and community that pour into you.

- **Set Standards & Boundaries:** Know what you want in a relationship before you get into one.

- **Enjoy Your Life:** Find joy, hobbies, and passions that make you feel fulfilled now.

Matthew 6:33 (NLT):

"Seek the Kingdom of God above all else, and live righteously, and he will give you everything you need."

Practical Exercises

1. **Write a Singleness Purpose Statement:** What do you want to accomplish in this season before entering a relationship?

2. **List Your Non-Negotiables:** Write down the core values you want in a partner, so you don't compromise in the future.

3. **Try Something New:** Travel, take a class, or start a passion project expand your world.

Journal Reflection
- Am I embracing my singleness or simply enduring it?
- How can I use this time to grow spiritually, emotionally, and mentally?
- What is one thing I can do today to invest in myself?

Closing Thoughts
Singleness is not a curse. It is not a delay. It is a gift—an opportunity to build a life you love before sharing it with someone else. Instead of rushing to the next season, embrace the one you're in. Who are you becoming in your singleness?

Chapter 5: Dating with Intention – Building Relationships That Last

Why Intentional Dating Matters

Many of us grew up watching our parents and grandparents follow certain dating traditions that simply don't work in today's culture. Times have changed. Traditional dating rules are outdated, but God's wisdom remains timeless.

Dating today can feel like an endless cycle of talking stages, ghosting, and situationships that leave people confused and emotionally drained. But intentional dating is different it's about clarity, purpose, and direction. If you don't date with intention, you'll waste time on people who were never meant to be in your life long-term.

Be Real Moment:
We live in a world where people avoid labels, keep their options open, and treat relationships like disposable items. Many are afraid of commitment because they don't want to lose their freedom. But here's the truth: if someone isn't serious about committing, they're not serious about loving you.

Intentional dating means being clear about what you want and being bold enough to walk away from what doesn't align with your values.

Proverbs 4:26 (NLT):
"Mark out a straight path for your feet; stay on the safe path."

What Dating with Intention Looks Like

- **Clarity:** You know why you're dating and what you're looking for.

- **Boundaries:** You set clear emotional, physical, and spiritual boundaries.

- **Commitment:** You're not afraid to define the relationship and make it official.

- **Spiritual Alignment:** You seek someone who shares your faith and values.

- **Emotional Maturity:** You're dating to build, not just to have fun.

Dating intentionally isn't about being rigid or overly serious it's about making sure your time, energy, and emotions are invested wisely.

Think About It: The Relationship That Went Nowhere
I once knew someone who spent years in a relationship that had no clear direction. She and her boyfriend never talked about the future, marriage, or real commitment. She hoped that one day he would "figure it out" and finally be ready to take the next step. He never did.

She eventually realized that she had been investing in a relationship with no foundation. She had ignored the red flags, hoping love alone would be enough to create a future. But love without intentionality is just wasted time.

If a relationship has no direction, it will lead to nowhere.

Amos 3:3 (NIV):
"Do two walk together unless they have agreed to do so?"

How to Date with Intention in Today's World

- **Be Clear About Your Goals:** Are you dating for fun, or are you seeking a future spouse? Be honest with yourself and your potential partner.

- **Ask the Right Questions Early:** Don't wait years to discuss faith, marriage, and values.

- **Look for Consistency, Not Just Chemistry:** Chemistry fades, but consistency builds trust.

- **Set Boundaries to Protect Your Heart:** Emotional and physical boundaries keep the relationship healthy.

- **Be Willing to Walk Away:** If the relationship is not aligned with your values, leaving is better than settling.

Matthew 6:33 (NLT):
"Seek the Kingdom of God above all else, and live righteously, and he will give you everything you need."

Practical Exercises

1. **Write Your Dating Intentions:** What are you looking for in a relationship? Be clear and specific.

2. **List Your Relationship Non-Negotiables:** What are the values and traits you won't compromise on?

3. **Assess Your Current Dating Habits:** Are your dating patterns leading you toward the type of relationship you desire?

Journal Reflection

- Am I dating with purpose, or am I just going with the flow?

- Do my dating habits reflect my values and long-term goals?

- What changes do I need to make in how I approach relationships?

Closing Thoughts

Dating with intention doesn't mean rushing into marriage it means being intentional about who you give your time, heart, and energy to. Don't waste your life on relationships that lead nowhere. Date with clarity. Date with purpose. Date with wisdom. Are you building something real, or are you just passing time?

Chapter 6: Are You Really Ready to Be a Spouse?

The Weight of Commitment

Most people love the IDEA of marriage, but do they truly understand the weight of commitment that comes with it? Marriage is not just a celebration, a pretty ring, or a well-curated Instagram post it is a covenant that requires responsibility, maturity, and a heart to serve.

Too often, people rush into relationships without first asking themselves, AM I REALLY READY? But the real question isn't just if you're ready to get married it's, are you ready to be a husband or wife?

Being a spouse is more than sharing a home, a bank account, or a last name. It's about stepping into a lifelong role of sacrifice, partnership, and leadership with another person.

Luke 14:28 (NLT):
"But don't begin until you count the cost. For who would begin construction of a building without first calculating the cost to see if there is enough money to finish it?"

Before saying "I do," take a moment to count the cost. Are you emotionally, spiritually, and mentally prepared for the demands of marriage?

Heart Truth: The Two Builders
This reminds me of the story of two men Jake and Jordan both eager to build their dream homes. Jake, a wise and patient man, spent months laying a solid foundation, ensuring the structure would withstand any storm. Jordan, in contrast, was eager to move in quickly and skipped the foundational work, rushing to build walls and add decor.

When the first heavy storm came, Jake's home stood firm, unmoved by the winds and floods. Jordan's house, however, collapsed. With no foundation, everything he worked for crumbled in an instant.

Marriage is much like these two homes. If you build on a strong foundation of wisdom, preparation, and commitment, your relationship will endure the storms of life. But if you rush in without spiritual, emotional, or financial stability, you risk watching everything fall apart.

Matthew 7:24-27 (ESV):

"Everyone then who hears these words of mine and does them will be like a wise man who built his house on the rock. And the rain fell, and the floods came, and the winds blew and beat on that house, but it did not fall, because it had been founded on the rock. And everyone who hears these words of mine and does not do them will be like a foolish man who built his house on the sand. And the rain fell, and the floods came, and the winds blew and beat against that house, and it fell, and great was the fall of it."

What kind of foundation are you building for your future marriage?

Marriage is About Giving, Not Just Getting

One of the biggest misconceptions about marriage is that it will fill your emptiness or solve your loneliness. But marriage isn't about completing each other it's about COMPLEMENTING one another.

If you're entering a relationship only thinking about what you will receive rather than what you can give, then you're not ready. Marriage is about serving, not just being served.

- Are you prepared to love unconditionally?

- Are you willing to make sacrifices for the good of your relationship?

- Are you emotionally mature enough to handle conflict without shutting down or retaliating?

Philippians 2:4 (NLT):
"Don't look out only for your own interests, but take an interest in others, too."

Real love requires selflessness. If you're still struggling with selfish tendencies, it's time to let God work on your heart before stepping into marriage.

-My Real-Life Moment: When My Spirit Said No

I remember the moment clearly; I was asked to be married. With my mouth, I said **yes**, but deep inside, my spirit said no.
It wasn't that he was a bad person. On paper, everything made sense. He loved me, he wanted to commit, and in many ways, I should have been excited. But something inside me the still, small voice of God was telling me that this was not my covenant partner.

The weight of that unspoken "no" sat heavy on my heart, even as I tried to convince myself otherwise. I thought, MAYBE I'M JUST SCARED. MAYBE I'M OVERTHINKING IT. But deep down, I knew that peace was missing. And when God isn't in something, He speaks loudest through the absence of peace.
Saying yes with my mouth but no in my spirit would have led me into a marriage where I was unequally yoked not just spiritually, but emotionally and in purpose. And let's be real: the wrong relationship, no matter how beautiful it looks on the outside, will always feel like a prison on the inside.

Choosing to walk away was painful, but it was also freeing. It reminded me that a temporary heartbreak is better than a lifetime of regret.

If you're on the verge of marriage, don't just check the external boxes. Check in with your spirit. God's voice will never contradict His peace.

Signs That You May Not Be Ready for Marriage

If you're unsure whether you're ready to be a spouse, here are some red flags that may indicate you need more time to prepare:

1. **You struggle with accountability.** If you reject correction and don't take responsibility for your actions, marriage will be a rough ride.

2. **You lack financial responsibility.** Marriage isn't just about love it's also about building a life together. If you can't manage your own money, you're not ready to handle shared finances.

3. **You run from conflict.** Do you shut down, avoid hard conversations, or explode in anger? If so, communication in marriage will be difficult.

4. **You have unhealed wounds from past relationships.** Bringing unhealed trauma into marriage will cause unnecessary struggles. Work on healing first.

5. **You believe marriage will fix you.** If you think a spouse will solve all your problems, you're setting yourself up for disappointment. Only God can heal and fulfill you.

Proverbs 24:27 (NLT):
"Do your planning and prepare your fields before building your house." Marriage is **not the foundation** you are. Build yourself first before trying to build a marriage.

Friendships as Preparation for Marriage
If you really want to know if you're ready for marriage, look at how you handle your friendships. Do you:

- Show up for your friends consistently, or only when it benefits you?

- Forgive and work through issues, or cut people off easily?

- Communicate openly, or avoid difficult conversations?

Proverbs 17:17 (NLT):

"A friend is always loyal, and a brother is born to help in time of need". How you handle your friendships reflects how you will handle your marriage. If you can't sustain long-term, meaningful friendships, how will you handle a lifelong commitment to a spouse?

Closing Thoughts

Marriage is a calling, not just a desire. It's a lifelong commitment that requires preparation, self-awareness, and a willingness to grow. If you're serious about being a spouse, take the time now to prepare, heal, and mature.

A healthy marriage starts with a healthy you. So, before you walk down the aisle, make sure you're truly ready to be a husband or wife.

Chapter 7: What You Inherit When You Become One

My Perspective: Marriage is More Than Love, It's Legacy

I believe, marriage is not just about love it's about legacy, family, and responsibility. I've watched couples step into marriage believing love alone is enough, only to find out that love doesn't pay bills, resolve conflicts, or automatically create unity.

Marriage is the merging of two lives, two families, and two histories into one. You don't just marry a person, you marry their background, their traditions, and their baggage. And they marry yours too.

The real question is, are you ready for what you inherit?

Genesis 2:24 (NIV):
"That is why a man leaves his father and mother and is united to his wife, and they become one flesh."

Becoming one is not just a spiritual bond it has real-life implications.

What You Gain When You Become One
- **A New Family:** Marriage ties you to your spouse's family, traditions, and history.
- **New Responsibilities:** You are no longer making decisions just for yourself.
- **A New Spiritual Weight:** Your marriage now carries spiritual responsibility before God.

- **A New Set of Challenges:** Conflict resolution, finances, and emotional growth become shared work.

Marriage is not just about a wedding day it's about building a life together.

Think About It: The Joined Households
Imagine two families living in separate houses. One day, a couple decides to unite their lives and build a bigger home. They each bring furniture, heirlooms, and traditions from their original houses. But when they move in together, they realize some things don't fit.

The husband's bulky antique furniture clashes with the wife's modern décor. The wife's loud, lively family visits often, while the husband prefers quiet evenings. Both are frustrated. They expected their new home to feel seamless, but instead, it requires adjustment, compromise, and blending.

This is exactly what happens in marriage. You are bringing your past, habits, and family culture into one space. You must decide what to keep, what to adjust, and what to leave behind.

Ephesians 4:2-3 (NLT):

"Always be humble and gentle. Be patient with each other, making allowance for each other's faults because of your love. Make every effort to keep yourselves united in the Spirit, binding yourselves together with peace."

Unity does not mean uniformity. It means learning how to blend two different lives in peace and love.

What You Must Let Go Of

Just as you gain new things in marriage, you must also be willing to release old things that no longer serve your covenant. This may include:

✖ **Unhealthy family patterns:** If your family history includes toxic behaviours, you must choose a new way.

✖ **Selfish independence:** Marriage requires partnership, not individualism.

✖ **Unforgiveness:** Past wounds will poison your marriage if you don't heal them first.

✖ **Emotional immaturity:** You must grow in patience, compromise, and understanding.

Letting go is not losing, it's making room for something greater.

How to Honor What You Inherit

1. **Honor Your Spouse's Background:** Be open to their family traditions and perspectives.
2. **Create New Family Values:** Decide together what habits, beliefs, and traditions will shape your new household.
3. **Commit to Growth:** Marriage is not about perfection— it's about progress.

Colossians 3:14 (ESV):
"And above all these put on love, which binds everything together in perfect harmony."

Harmony does not happen by accident it is chosen daily.

Practical Exercises

1. **Write a Family Inventory:** List the habits, traditions, and mindsets from both your family and your spouse's. Discuss what to keep, blend, or leave behind.

2. **Set New Family Values:** Together, write five core values that will define your marriage and future family.

3. **Practice Compromise:** Identify one area where you and your partner have different habits. Discuss a middle ground that works for both of you.

Journal Reflection

- What parts of my personal history will I carry into marriage?

- What traditions or habits will I need to adjust in order to build unity?

- How can I honor my spouse's background while maintaining my own identity?

Closing Thoughts

Marriage is not just a relationship it's an inheritance of love, responsibility, and legacy. When you say, "I do," you are choosing to embrace everything that comes with your spouse, just as they are embracing all of you.

The beauty of marriage is not in sameness, but in unity. The real work is learning to build a life that honors both of your pasts while forging a new, God-centered future.

Chapter 8: Mommy & Daddy Issues – Healing Before Marriage

How Your Parental Wounds Shape Your Relationships

Whether we realize it or not, our relationships with our parents shape how we love, trust, and communicate in our romantic relationships. **Unhealed wounds from childhood don't disappear when you start dating, they follow you.**

We all know people who have walked into relationships unaware that they are carrying emotional baggage from their parents. They say they want love but are afraid of intimacy. They crave stability but unconsciously sabotage healthy relationships.

If we don't take time to heal, we will unknowingly repeat the cycles we saw growing up.

The choices of past generations can impact families for years, but through God's grace, healing and restoration are possible. While generational patterns can influence us, we are not prisoners to them. We have the ability to break cycles, heal from past wounds, and create a new legacy rooted in faith, wisdom, and love.

You are **not** responsible for what happened in your past, but you are responsible for how you move forward.

Common Parental Wounds & Their Impact on Relationships

- **Absent Parent (Physically or Emotionally):** You may struggle with rejection, abandonment issues, or people pleasing.

- **Overly Critical Parent:** You might feel like nothing you do is ever enough, making you crave validation in relationships.

- **Emotionally Unavailable Parent:** You may have difficulty expressing feelings or trusting others with your emotions.

- **Toxic or Controlling Parent:** You might struggle with fear of failure, independence issues, or rebellion.

- **Divorced or Unstable Household:** You may fear commitment or believe love is always temporary.

These wounds don't just disappear. They must be addressed, processed, and healed.

Think About It: The Cracked Mirror
Imagine looking into a mirror that has cracks all over it. No matter how beautiful you are, the reflection is always distorted. That's what unhealed wounds do to your relationships.

When you don't heal, you don't see love clearly. You interpret your partner's actions through the lens of your pain, assuming rejection when there's none, or pushing away love because you're afraid to be vulnerable.

Psalm 147:3 (NIV):
"He heals the brokenhearted and binds up their wounds."
Healing starts with acknowledging the cracks then letting God restore your vision.

Healing Before Marriage
Marriage is not a cure for emotional wounds. If anything, it magnifies them.

Here's how to start healing before stepping into a covenant relationship:

- **Identify the Root:** Take time to reflect on how your childhood shaped your view of love, trust, and intimacy.

- **Forgive (Even If They Don't Apologize):** Forgiveness is not about excusing behaviours it's about freeing yourself from its grip.

- **Seek Wise Counsel:** Therapy, mentorship, or pastoral guidance can help unpack deep wounds.

- **Rebuild Your Self-Worth:** Your identity should be rooted in who God says you are, not in how your parents treated you.

- **Break the Cycle:** Be intentional about not repeating toxic patterns in your own relationships and future family.

Isaiah 61:3 (ESV):

"To grant to those who mourn in Zion to give them a beautiful headdress instead of ashes, the oil of gladness instead of mourning, the garment of praise instead of a faint spirit."

God wants to exchange your past pain for His healing.

Practical Exercises

1. **Write a Letter (But Don't Send It):** Express everything you've ever wanted to say to your parent(s). Let it be raw and honest.

2. **List the Patterns:** Identify relationship habits that you may have inherited from your parents. Are they healthy or unhealthy?

3. **Pray for Emotional Healing:** Ask God to heal your wounds and help you create a new legacy for your future marriage.

Journal Reflection

- How have my parents' actions (or inactions) shaped my view of love and commitment?

- What areas of my heart still need healing before I enter marriage?

- How can I invite God into my healing process?

Closing Thoughts

Your past does not define your future. You have the power to break generational cycles, to heal, and to love differently.
Healing is a process, but when you allow God to do the work in you, you enter relationships whole, secure, and ready to love in a way that reflects His design.

Will you take the time to heal before stepping into love?

Chapter 9: Healthy Ways to Respond to Loneliness

Loneliness vs. Being Alone

There's a difference between being alone and feeling lonely. Being alone can be peaceful, necessary, and even healing, but loneliness is the ache that tells us something is missing. The problem isn't the absence of people; it's the absence of meaningful connection.

Loneliness doesn't just affect singles it affects married people, people in relationships, and even those surrounded by friends and family. The question isn't how do I stop being lonely? but how do I handle loneliness in a way that makes me stronger?

Psalm 68:6 (NLT):
"God places the lonely in families; he sets the prisoners free and gives them joy. But he makes the rebellious live in a sun-scorched land."

God never intended for us to do life alone. But before we rush to fill loneliness with distractions, relationships, or busyness, we need to understand what it's teaching us.

Why We Feel Lonely
Loneliness isn't just about physical isolation. It's deeper than that.

We can feel lonely when:

- We don't feel seen or understood

- We lack genuine connections

- We're going through a season of transition

- We're disconnected from God's presence

- We've attached our worth to romantic relationships

Loneliness is often a call to self discovery and deeper faith. If we allow it, it can push us toward growth instead of emptiness.

Think about it: The Withering Tree

A young woman had a tree in her backyard that started losing leaves and drying up. She assumed it was dying, but after some research, she realized it wasn't the tree that was the problem it was the soil. The tree needed deeper roots and richer nutrients to thrive again.

Loneliness can feel like that withering tree but it's not always a sign that something is wrong with us. It may just mean we need deeper roots in God, better self-care, and stronger relationships. Instead of treating loneliness like something to escape, treat it like something to learn from.

John 15:5 (NIV):

"I am the vine; you are the branches. If you remain in me and I in you, you will bear much fruit; apart from me you can do nothing."

Healthy Ways to Respond to Loneliness

- **Deepen Your Relationship with God:** Use this time to pray, read scripture, and worship.

- **Strengthen Friendships:** Invest in godly friendships that uplift and encourage you.

- **Develop Your Purpose:** Loneliness is often a signal to focus on your calling, dreams, and growth.

- **Serve Others:** Sometimes, the best way to overcome loneliness is to pour into others.

- **Prioritize Self-Care:** Take care of your mental, emotional, and physical well-being.

What NOT to Do When You're Lonely

✖ **Rush into a relationship out of desperation**

✖ **Use social media to compare your life to others**

✖ **Numb yourself with distractions (Streaming, social media, food, work, etc.)**

✖ **Dwell in self-pity instead of taking action**

Loneliness is an invitation, not a punishment. It's a call to growth, intimacy with God, and deeper self-awareness.

Practical Exercises

1. **Journaling Exercise:** Write about a time you felt lonely. What did you learn from that season?

2. **Connection Challenge:** Reach out to someone you admire spiritually and ask to meet for coffee or prayer.

3. **Bible Study Plan:** Choose a book of the Bible (like Psalms or Ecclesiastes) and study how biblical figures handled loneliness.

Journal Reflection

- How do I typically handle loneliness?

- What can I do differently to embrace solitude instead of fearing it?

- How can I use this season to grow closer to God and others?

Closing Thoughts

Loneliness is not a curse it's an opportunity. Instead of letting it drive you toward unhealthy choices, let it drive you toward wholeness, purpose, and stronger faith.

Embrace the season you're in. God is using it to shape you for something greater.

Chapter 10: Sex & Purity – God's Design for Intimacy

Sex is More Than Physical

The world often treats sex as casual, recreational, and purely physical, but God designed it to be sacred, covenantal, and deeply spiritual. Sex is not just about pleasure it's about connection, oneness, and responsibility.

From what I have observed, many people enter relationships thinking that sex is just another part of dating. But I've also seen the emotional, spiritual, and psychological damage that comes when sex is misused outside of God's intended design.

Sex is powerful. It creates bonds, forges attachments, and carries spiritual weight. This is why God placed boundaries around it—not to withhold good things from us, but to protect us from harm.

1 Corinthians 6:18-20 (NIV):
"Flee from sexual immorality. All other sins a person commits are outside the body, but whoever sins sexually, sins against their own body. Do you not know that your bodies are temples of the Holy Spirit, who is in you, whom you have received from God? You are not your own; you were bought at a price. Therefore, honor God with your bodies."

Sex isn't just about your body it's about your soul, mind, and spirit too.

Purity is More Than Abstinence!

Purity is often misunderstood as simply abstaining from sex until marriage, but purity is much deeper than that. You can be a virgin and still struggle with impurity in your thoughts, desires, and entertainment choices. Purity isn't just about what you do with your body it's about the condition of your heart and mind.

- Purity is about self-control and discipline.

- Purity protects your heart from unnecessary heartbreak.

- Purity strengthens your relationship with God.

- Purity builds trust and self-discipline for marriage.

- Purity allows for clarity, you can make wise decisions without being clouded by physical intimacy.

Let's be real there are people who aren't even in committed relationships but are still hooking up with their "homies" just for convenience. That's a whole different headache that we don't even have time to deal with here!

Purity is about intentionality not just avoiding sex, but setting healthy boundaries in your relationships, mind, and lifestyle.

Matthew 5:8 (ESV):
"Blessed are the pure in heart, for they shall see God."

Think About It: The Fire in the Fireplace

Imagine a fire. In the right place inside a fireplace, it brings warmth, comfort, and beauty. But if you take that same fire and light, it in the middle of your living room, it can burn the whole house down.

Sex is like fire. Within marriage, it strengthens, bonds, and deepens love. Outside of marriage, it can lead to heartbreak, confusion, and regret.

If your partner is truly your forever person, you will have forever to enjoy intimacy with them. So what's the rush? Rushing into sex before marriage often clouds judgment and builds relationships on temporary pleasure rather than lasting commitment.

Song of Solomon 8:4 (NIV):
"Daughters of Jerusalem, I charge you: Do not arouse or awaken love until it so desires."

God's boundaries are not to restrict us, they are to protect us

Healing from Sexual Sin

If you've made mistakes in this area, know this: God's grace is bigger than your past. Purity is not about being perfect it's about choosing to walk in a new direction.

- Acknowledge where you need healing.

- Pray for God's restoration and renewal.

- Set new boundaries that honor your future.

- Surround yourself with accountability.

Psalm 51:10 (NLT):
"Create in me a clean heart, O God. Renew a loyal spirit within me."

Practical Exercises

1. **Heart Check:** Write down your personal beliefs about sex and purity. Compare them with what God says in His Word.

2. **Accountability Partner:** Find someone who can help you stay committed to your purity journey.

3. **Set Clear Boundaries:** Identify areas where you need to establish stronger boundaries in dating.

Journal Reflection

- How has my perspective on sex and purity been shaped by culture vs. faith?

- What boundaries do I need to set to protect my heart and relationship with God?

- How can I invite God into my journey of purity and healing?

Closing Thoughts

Sex was never meant to be casual it was meant to be covenantal. When we understand God's design, we can walk in freedom, clarity, and wholeness.

If you've struggled in this area, know that God's grace is available to you. Purity is not just about waiting for marriage it's about living in a way that honors God every day.

Will you trust Him with this area of your life?

Chapter 11: Unforgiveness – The Silent Relationship Killer

How Unforgiveness Poisons Relationships

Unforgiveness is one of the most dangerous silent killers in relationships. It may not always be visible at first, but over time, it corrodes trust, intimacy, and peace. Many relationships don't fail because of a lack of love but because of resentment that was never dealt with.

The truth is, some bring unforgiveness into relationships thinking they can hide it. But wounds that go unhealed don't stay buried they resurface in the way we react, communicate, and even love.

Be Real Moment:
Forgiveness is easier said than done. Sometimes the pain is deep, the betrayal feels unforgivable, and the person who hurt us doesn't even acknowledge the damage they caused. But holding onto unforgiveness doesn't protect us it only keeps us bound to the hurt.

Ephesians 4:31-32 (NLT):
"Get rid of all bitterness, rage, anger, harsh words, and slander, as well as all types of evil behavior. Instead, be kind to each other, tenderhearted, forgiving one another, just as God through Christ has forgiven you."

Unforgiveness doesn't just affect your past, it can destroy your future.

The Weight of Holding On

When we refuse to forgive, we carry emotional baggage that affects everything:

- **Communication:** Unhealed resentment can make us defensive, guarded, or passive aggressive.

- **Trust:** The more hurt we carry, the harder it is to trust others with our hearts.

- **Emotional Health:** Unforgiveness leads to stress, anxiety, and even physical illness.

- **Spiritual Growth:** A bitter heart creates distance between us and God.

Holding on to past hurt is like drinking poison and expecting the other person to suffer.

Matthew 6:14-15 (NIV):
"For if you forgive other people when they sin against you, your heavenly Father will also forgive you. But if you do not forgive others their sins, your father will not forgive your sins."

Unforgiveness is not just about them it's about your own freedom.

Think About It: The Heavy Suitcase

Imagine carrying a suitcase filled with bricks. Every brick represents an offense, a wound, or a betrayal. Over time, the suitcase becomes heavier, and no matter where you go, it weighs you down.

That's what unforgiveness does. It slows you down, drains your energy, and affects your ability to move forward.
Now, imagine dropping that suitcase and walking away. That's the power of forgiveness—it releases you.

Colossians 3:13 (ESV):
"Bear with each other and forgive one another if any of you has a grievance against someone. Forgive as the Lord forgave you."

Forgiveness is not weakness. It is strength in action.

How to Truly Forgive

- **Acknowledge the Hurt:** You can't heal what you don't admit. Be honest about how you feel.

- **Release the Need for Revenge:** Letting go doesn't mean excusing the offense, it means choosing peace over bitterness.

- **Pray for Healing:** Ask God to help you forgive, even when you don't feel like it.

- **Set Boundaries (If Necessary):** Forgiveness doesn't always mean reconciliation, it means releasing the burden.

- **Choose Freedom Daily:** Forgiveness is not a one-time act. It's a daily decision to let go and move forward.

Isaiah 43:18-19 (NIV):
"Forget the former things; do not dwell on the past. See, I am doing a new thing! Now it springs up; do you not perceive it? I am making a way in the wilderness and streams in the wasteland." God wants to do something new in your life—but you must be willing to let go of the old.

Practical Exercises

1. **Write a Forgiveness Letter:** Write a letter (but don't send it) to the person who hurt you. Release the pain in writing.

2. **Identify Your Baggage:** Make a list of past hurts you're still carrying. Pray over each one, asking God to help you let go.

3. **Daily Affirmations:** Speak this daily: I CHOOSE TO FORGIVE. I RELEASE MY PAST. I AM FREE FROM BITTERNESS AND PAIN.

Journal Reflection

- Who do I need to forgive, and what's stopping me?

- How has holding onto pain affected my relationships?

- What steps can I take today to walk in freedom?

Closing Thoughts

Forgiveness is not about them, it's about you. It's about choosing peace, breaking free from the past, and allowing God to heal your heart. You cannot build a healthy relationship with unresolved pain. If you want love, joy, and peace in your future, you must be willing to let go of the past.

Are you ready to release the weight and walk in freedom?

Chapter 12: Healing – Overcoming the Past

The Power of Healing Before Love

Healing is often overlooked in conversations about relationships, but a healthy love life starts with a healed heart. Too many people jump into relationships hoping someone else will fix their brokenness, only to find that pain doesn't disappear it multiplies when left unaddressed.

I've seen it happen. People walk into love carrying unhealed wounds from childhood, past relationships, or personal struggles. Instead of experiencing joy, they end up projecting their fears, insecurities, and past hurts onto their partners. But love is not meant to be a bandage it is meant to be a partnership.

Be Real Moment:

Healing isn't easy. It takes time, effort, and facing things we would rather ignore. But avoiding your wounds doesn't make them go away it only makes them stronger, deeper, and harder to control. True healing requires honesty, self-awareness, and a willingness to let God in.

If you don't deal with your past, your past will deal with you.

Psalm 147:3 (NIV):
"He heals the brokenhearted and binds up their wounds."

Signs You Still Need Healing

- **You struggle with trust.** Past betrayals have made you fearful of being hurt again.

- **You get triggered easily.** Small disagreements turn into emotional breakdowns because old wounds still linger.

- **You look for validation in relationships.** Your self-worth is tied to how others treat you.

- **You have unresolved anger.** You find yourself bitter toward people who remind you of past pain.

- **You sabotage good things.** When things are going well, you create conflict out of fear of getting hurt.

Recognizing these signs is not a failure, it's an invitation to heal.

Think About It: Empty

I had a good friend who was dating a well-known recording artist. On the surface, she had everything glamorous trips, VIP access, and financial security. But despite the glitz and public admiration, she confided in me that she felt empty, unseen, and emotionally exhausted.

She thought this relationship would fill the void she had carried since childhood created by abandonment issues and deep-seated insecurities. Instead, the cracks in her foundation only widened. No matter how much love and attention she received, it was never enough because she hadn't healed from her past wounds.

One day, she broke down and admitted, "I keep thinking if I can just be enough, he'll finally love me the way I need. But I'm realizing it's not about him it's about me not being whole within myself."

That moment shifted everything for her. She realized a relationship cannot heal what only God can. She had to step away, prioritize her healing, and learn to love herself outside of the validation of another person.

Isaiah 61:1 (ESV):
"The Spirit of the Lord God is upon me, because the Lord has anointed me to bring good news to the poor; he has sent me to bind up the brokenhearted, to proclaim liberty to the captives, and the opening of the prison to those who are bound."

Steps to Healing Through Faith

- **Acknowledge the Pain:** Healing starts with honesty. What wounds are you still carrying?

- **Surrender It to God:** Pray and invite Him into your healing process.

- **Forgive Yourself and Others:** Let go of guilt, shame, and resentment.

- **Seek Support:** Whether through therapy, mentorship, or a trusted community, healing is not meant to be done alone.

- **Replace Lies with Truth:** The enemy wants you to believe you're broken beyond repair, but God says you are redeemed and restored.

2 Corinthians 5:17 (NLT):
"This means that anyone who belongs to Christ has become a new person. The old life is gone; a new life has begun!"

—

Practical Exercises

1. **Write Your Healing Story:** What experiences have shaped you? Where do you still need healing?

2. **Create a Prayer Plan:** Dedicate time to pray specifically over your emotional wounds.

3. **Speak Life Over Yourself:** Write affirmations based on Scripture and repeat them daily.

Journal Reflection

- What wounds am I still carrying, and how have they impacted my relationships?

- What steps can I take today to invite God into my healing journey?

- How will healing change the way I love and receive love?

Closing Thoughts

Healing isn't just about moving on it's about becoming whole. Before you enter love, take time to let God heal your heart. The healthier you are, the healthier your future relationships will be. Will you allow God to make you whole before you give yourself away?

Chapter 13: The Importance of Emotional Maturity in Relationships

Why Emotional Maturity Matters

Many relationships struggle not because of a lack of love, but because of a lack of emotional maturity. Love alone cannot sustain a healthy relationship maturity is required.

Emotional maturity is the ability to handle conflict, communicate effectively, and take responsibility for your own emotions without projecting them onto your partner. Without it, relationships become filled with misunderstandings, unnecessary drama, and cycles of emotional highs and lows.

Let's Be Real Moment
We've all seen people jump from relationship to relationship, blaming their ex every time something goes wrong. But at some point, we have to ask, "am I the common denominator?"

Emotional maturity means owning your growth, not just pointing fingers. You can't expect a mature relationship if you're still responding to conflict with childish reactions.

Proverbs 19:11 (NIV):
"A person's wisdom yields patience; it is to one's glory to overlook an offense."

Signs of Emotional Maturity in a Relationship

- **You Take Responsibility for Your Actions:** You don't blame your partner for everything.

- **You Communicate Clearly & Respectfully:** You express your needs without manipulation or passive-aggressiveness.

- **You Can Handle Conflict Without Exploding or Shutting Down:** You don't run from difficult conversations.

- **You Have Healthy Boundaries:** You know how to say no without feeling guilty.

- **You Control Your Emotions, Not the Other Way Around:** You don't let temporary feelings dictate permanent decisions.

- **You Choose Growth Over Comfort:** You seek to improve yourself instead of making excuses for toxic behaviours.

Without emotional maturity, even the best relationship will eventually crumble under pressure.

Think About It: The Relationship That Wasn't Ready
There was a couple who had deep love for each other but couldn't stop arguing. Every disagreement turned into a battle of pride instead of a conversation for understanding. Neither of them was willing to listen, compromise, or admit when they were wrong.

Eventually, love wasn't enough to keep them together.
They realized that a relationship without emotional maturity will always feel exhausting.

James 1:19 (NLT):
"Understand this, my dear brothers and sisters: You must all be quick to listen, slow to speak, and slow to get angry."

How to Grow in Emotional Maturity

- **Self-Reflection:** Take time to evaluate how you handle stress, emotions, and conflict.

- **Develop Emotional Intelligence:** Learn to recognize and control your own feelings before reacting impulsively.

- **Practice Active Listening:** Instead of preparing your response, actually hear what the other person is saying.

- **Own Your Mistakes:** Maturity means saying "I WAS WRONG" without making excuses.

- **Heal from Past Trauma:** Unresolved wounds can cause you to react irrationally in relationships. Seek healing.

- **Surround Yourself with Emotionally Mature People:** Growth happens in the right environment.

Colossians 3:13 (NLT):
"Make allowance for each other's faults and forgive anyone who offends you. Remember, the Lord forgave you, so you must forgive others."

Practical Exercises

1. **Journal Your Emotional Triggers:** Identify what situations make you react emotionally.

2. **Practice Responding Instead of Reacting:** Next time you're upset, take a deep breath before answering.

3. **Apologize Without Justifying:** If you've wronged someone, say "I'M SORRY" without adding, "BUT YOU MADE ME DO IT."

Journal Reflection

- How do I handle conflict in relationships?

- What areas of emotional maturity do I need to work on?

- How can I become a better communicator in my relationships?

Closing Thoughts

Emotional maturity isn't just about what you want in a partner it's about who you are becoming.

Before praying for a mature relationship, ask yourself: Am I emotionally ready for the love I desire?

Chapter 14: The Impact of Social Media on Relationships

How Social Media Has Changed Dating

Social media has redefined relationships. From Instagram posts to dating apps, we live in a time where love is often measured in likes, comments, and DMs. But while social media connects us, it can also create unrealistic expectations, distractions, and insecurities.

If not used wisely, social media can become a silent threat to a healthy relationship.

Be Real Moment:

We've all seen those PERFECT couples on social media—the ones who seem to have it all together. But let's be real: social media is a highlight reel, not real life.

Comparison will rob you of contentment if you're not careful. If your relationship is built on appearances rather than authenticity, it will eventually crumble.

Proverbs 4:23 (NLT):
"Guard your heart above all else, for it determines the course of your life."

The Pros and Cons of Social Media in Dating

✓ **Pros:**

- Allows for easy communication and connection.
- Can be a great tool for meeting like-minded people.
- Encourages public affirmation in relationships.

✖ Cons:

- Creates unrealistic relationship standards.
- Encourages comparison and insecurity.
- Can lead to temptation, emotional cheating, and lack of privacy.

A healthy relationship isn't defined by social media it's built offline through trust, communication, and commitment.

Think About It: The 'Perfect' Online Couple

I once knew a couple who looked perfect online. Matching outfits, romantic getaways, and endless 'couple goals' captions. But behind closed doors, their relationship was falling apart. They were more focused on how they looked to the world than how they actually treated each other.
One day, they ended things but instead of grieving the breakup, they were more concerned with how to ANNOUNCE IT online.

Their relationship was built for the internet, not for real life.

Galatians 1:10 (NIV):
"Am I now trying to win the approval of human beings, or of God? Or am I trying to please people? If I were still trying to please people, I would not be a servant of Christ."

How to Protect Your Relationship from Social Media Drama

- **Prioritize Privacy:** Not everything needs to be shared online.

- **Don't Compare:** Just because a couple looks happy online doesn't mean they're thriving.

- **Set Boundaries:** Discuss what is and isn't appropriate regarding social media behaviour.

- **Be Mindful of Emotional Cheating:** Liking photos, DMing, or excessive interaction with someone else can cross boundaries.

- **Stay Present:** Don't let your phone distract you from real connection.

1 Corinthians 10:23 (NLT):
"You say, 'I am allowed to do anything' but not everything is good for you. You say, 'I am allowed to do anything' but not everything is beneficial."

Practical Exercises

1. **Social Media Detox Challenge:** Take a break from social media for a weekend and reflect on how it affects your mindset and relationships.

2. **Define Your Relationship Boundaries:** Have an honest conversation about how you and your partner will use social media.

3. **Unfollow for Mental Peace:** If certain accounts make you feel insecure, unfollow them and guard your peace.

Journal Reflection
- How has social media influenced my view of relationships?
- Do I compare my relationship to unrealistic online standards?
- What boundaries can I set to make sure social media doesn't negatively impact my love life?

Closing Thoughts
Social media is a tool, it can either strengthen your relationship or weaken it,
depending on how you use it.

Are you building something real, or just something that looks good online?

Chapter 15: The Role of Accountability in Relationships

Why Accountability is Essential for Healthy Love

The idea of accountability in relationships isn't talked about enough. In today's culture, independence is glorified, and people often think they don't need anyone to hold them accountable for their choices in dating and love. But the truth is, without accountability, relationships become a breeding ground for unchecked emotions, bad decisions, and avoidable heartbreak.

A relationship that is built without wise counsel, godly influence, and honest feedback is like trying to drive at night without headlights you may not realize you're headed for a crash until it's too late.

Be Real Moment:
Most of us have been in a situation where a friend or mentor tried to warn us about a relationship, but we didn't listen. Maybe they saw things we couldn't see, or maybe they recognized red flags that we brushed off. But accountability exists to protect us, not to control us.

Proverbs 11:14 (NIV):
"For lack of guidance a nation falls, but victory is won through many advisers."

Accountability is not about someone else running your relationship it's about surrounding yourself with people who want to see you thrive and who will call you out when you're about to mess up.

Who Should Hold You Accountable?

Not everyone should have a say in your relationship, but you should have a few trusted people who can speak wisdom into your life. Look for:

- **Godly Mentors** – People who have been in healthy relationships and can offer wisdom.

- **Close Friends Who Will Be Honest** – The ones who won't just tell you what you want to hear.

- **Spiritual Leaders/Pastors** – People who can provide biblical counsel and prayer support.

- **Yourself** – Yes, you also need to hold yourself accountable for your actions, choices, and mindset.

Think About It: The Person Who Didn't Listen
They were warned. Their friends pointed out concerning behaviors, their pastor suggested they slow down, and even their own intuition whispered that something wasn't right. But they ignored it all, convinced that their emotions were enough to sustain the relationship.
Fast forward a year, and they were heartbroken, saying "I SHOULD'VE LISTENED."

Accountability isn't about control it's about protection. A refusal to be accountable is a sign of pride, and pride always leads to a fall.

Proverbs 15:22 (NLT):
"Plans go wrong for lack of advice; many advisers bring success."

How to Embrace Accountability in Your Dating Life

- **Be Open to Correction** – If the only people you keep around are those who agree with you, you're setting yourself up for failure.

- **Check in with Your Mentors Regularly** – Ask for wisdom, prayer, and advice when navigating relationships.

- **Don't Date in Isolation** – A relationship that avoids community is a relationship that often hides something.

- **Listen to Red Flags from Trusted People** – If multiple people are saying the same thing about your relationship, don't ignore it.

- **Hold Yourself Accountable** – Be honest with yourself about your actions, choices, and whether you're honoring God in your relationship.

James 5:16 (ESV):
"Therefore, confess your sins to one another and pray for one another, that you may be healed. The prayer of a righteous person has great power as it is working."

Practical Exercises

1. **Identify Your Accountability Circle:** Who are three people who can speak into your dating life with wisdom and honesty?

2. **Have an Honest Conversation:** If you're currently in a relationship, ask a trusted mentor or friend for their honest thoughts.

3. **Set Relationship Check-Ins:** If you're dating, create a habit of checking in with a mentor or trusted friend every few weeks.

Journal Reflection

- Do I resist accountability, or do I welcome it?

- Who are the people in my life that I trust to speak wisdom into my relationships?

- How can I create a culture of accountability in my dating life moving forward?

Closing Thoughts

Accountability isn't about people telling you what to do it's about making sure you don't walk blindly into avoidable pain.

A healthy relationship isn't built in isolation. Who's in your corner making sure you're not settling, rushing, or walking into danger?

Chapter 16: Breaking Soul Ties & Emotional Attachments

What is a Soul Tie?

A soul tie is a deep emotional, physical, or spiritual connection with another person, often formed through intimate relationships. These connections can be healthy such as bonds between spouses or close friends or unhealthy, where they keep you emotionally bound to a past relationship, preventing growth and healing.

Many people walk away from relationships physically but remain **emotionally entangled** long after the breakup. You can delete their number, unfollow them, and avoid their social media, yet still feel mentally and emotionally stuck.

Be Real Moment
Have you ever found yourself thinking about someone years after the relationship ended? Maybe you compare every new person you date to them. Maybe a certain song or place brings back intense emotions. If so, you may still have a **soul tie** lingering.
Unhealthy soul ties can make you feel attached to someone who no longer serves your purpose or aligns with your future. It's time to break free.

1 Corinthians 6:18 (NLT):
"Run from sexual sin! No other sin so clearly affects the body as this one does. For sexual immorality is a sin against your own body."

Yikes! Can it get any clearer than that....

Signs You Have an Unhealthy Soul Tie

- You constantly think about them, even when you don't want to.

- You struggle to move forward in new relationships.

- You compare everyone to them.

- You feel emotionally or physically drawn back to them, even after they've hurt you.

- You still feel connected through dreams, emotions, or random urges to reach out.

- You have difficulty forgiving and letting go.

If you recognize any of these signs, it's time to break free.

Think About It: The Chain That Won't Break

Imagine walking through life dragging a heavy chain behind you. Each link represents an old emotional wound, a past relationship, or lingering attachment. Every step forward feels difficult because the weight is still attached to you. That's what an unhealthy soul tie does it holds you back from embracing what's ahead.

You cannot step into your future while being chained to your past.

Isaiah 43:18-19 (NIV):

"Forget the former things; do not dwell on the past. See, I am doing a new thing! Now it springs up; do you not perceive it? I am making a way in the wilderness and streams in the wasteland."

—

How to Break a Soul Tie

- **Acknowledge It:** Admit that this connection is unhealthy and is keeping you bound.

- **Repent (Turn away) & Ask for God's Help:** Soul ties are often rooted in sexual sin, emotional dependency, or idolatry. Ask God for forgiveness and healing.

- **Cut Off Communication:** Continuing to talk to them only strengthens the tie. Delete, block, and move on.

- **Renounce the Soul Tie:** Speak out loud that you are breaking the connection, cancelling any spiritual bond formed.

- **Pray & Fast:** Spiritual warfare requires spiritual discipline. Fasting and prayer are powerful tools in breaking free.

- **Replace the Void with God's Love:** Fill the empty space with worship, scripture, and godly relationships.

James 4:7 (NLT):
"So humble yourselves before God. Resist the devil, and he will flee from you."

Practical Exercises

1. **Write a Letter to Release Them:** Express everything you need to say, then rip it up as a symbol of letting go.

2. **Make a Clean Break:** Unfollow, delete photos, and remove anything that keeps you emotionally tied.

3. **Daily Affirmations for Freedom:** Speak life over yourself: "I am free from the past. my heart is whole. my future is blessed."

Journal Reflection
- What emotional attachments am I still holding onto?

- How is this affecting my ability to move forward?

- What steps will I take today to break free from unhealthy soul ties?

Closing Thoughts
Healing from soul ties doesn't happen overnight, but it does happen when you are intentional. You deserve to be free, whole, and emotionally available for the future God has for you.
Will you release what's behind you so you can fully embrace what's ahead?

Chapter 17: Trusting God's Timing – Patience in the Waiting

God's Plan vs. Your Timeline

It's easy to feel impatient when it seems like love is taking longer than expected. Culture tells us that by a certain age, we should have marriage, kids, and the perfect life. But God's plan doesn't run on human deadlines.

If you rush into the wrong relationship out of fear of waiting, you could end up delaying the right one. God's best often requires patience, and patience requires trust.

Heart Truth:
Waiting is hard. Seeing your friends get engaged while you're still figuring things out can be frustrating. It's tempting to settle just to keep up. But forced timing leads to forced relationships and nothing forced ever flows.
Trusting God means believing that delays are not denials. What He has for you will not pass you by.

Ecclesiastes 3:11 (NIV):
"He has made everything beautiful in its time. He has also set eternity in the human heart; yet no one can fathom what God has done from beginning to end."

Why God May Have You Waiting

- **Character Development:** God is shaping you into the person your future spouse needs.

- **Spiritual Growth:** This season may be about strengthening your relationship with Him.

- **Healing & Wholeness:** You might need to work through past wounds before stepping into marriage.

- **Protection:** God could be keeping you from something that isn't His best for you.

- **Divine Timing:** He is aligning circumstances, locations, and people in ways you can't see yet.

What looks like a delay is often divine preparation.

Think About It: The Job You Almost Took
Imagine being desperate for a job. You apply everywhere, and finally, an offer comes. It's not what you really wanted, but you take it out of fear that nothing better will come.
Months later, your dream job opens up but now you're stuck in a position that drains you.

That's what happens when you rush relationships. You can miss God's best by settling for what's available.
Trusting God's timing means believing that what He has for you is worth the wait.

Isaiah 40:31 (NLT):
"But those who trust in the Lord will find new strength. They will soar high on wings like eagles. They will run and not grow weary. They will walk and not faint."

—

How to Wait Well

- **Stop Comparing:** Your journey is unique. Don't measure it against someone else's timeline.

- **Focus on Purpose:** Use this season to grow spiritually, emotionally, and mentally.

- **Stay Open to God's Lead:** Be willing to walk away from anything that doesn't align with His plan.

- **Pray for Discernment:** Not every good opportunity is a God opportunity.

- **Find Joy in the Present:** Live a full life now instead of waiting for marriage to bring fulfillment.

Matthew 6:33 (NLT):
"Seek the Kingdom of God above all else, and live righteously, and he will give you everything you need."

Practical Exercises

1. **Write a Letter to Your Future Self:** Describe where you are now and what you hope to see in your future marriage.

2. **Identify Growth Areas:** List areas where you need development before stepping into a serious relationship.

3. **Make a Joy List:** Write down things that bring you happiness OUTSIDE of a relationship.

Journal Reflection
- Am I trusting God's timing, or am I trying to force my own?

- How can I embrace this season instead of rushing through it?

- What is one way I can grow spiritually, emotionally, or mentally while I wait?

Closing Thoughts

Delays are not rejections, they are often redirections. God's timing is never late, and His plans are never wrong.

Instead of stressing over when love will come, focus on becoming the person who is ready for it.

Will you trust that God's best is still ahead?

Chapter 18: Final Reflection – Knowing Ourselves

We're Not Alone

If we've made it to this point together, let's take a moment to acknowledge something we're not alone. Every story, example, and lesson in this book was written for us, to help us understand ourselves better and make sense of our relationships. Love, breakups, and personal growth are things we all experience, and no one has it all figured out.

Life, love, and self-discovery shape us in ways we don't always expect. But here's something important to remember: If you lost someone but found yourself, you didn't lose. You learned. You grew. And you took another step toward becoming who you're meant to be.

Heart Truth:
It's easy to think, "THEY SHOULD HAVE TRIED HARDER FOR ME." But a better question is, "DID WE MAKE THE BEST CHOICES FOR OURSELVES?" One mindset keeps us stuck in the past, while the other helps us move forward.
If we ever think that heartbreak or being single is a punishment it isn't.
It is a chance to grow. It is preparation.

Romans 8:28 (NLT):
"And we know that God causes everything to work together for the good of those who love God and are called according to his purpose for them."

This Book Is Based on Real Life
This book isn't just about theories it's about real lessons learned from experience.

We've seen people rush into relationships before they were ready. Some of us have stayed in relationships that made us unhappy because we were afraid of being alone. And we've had to make tough decisions about letting go, even when everything seemed like it should work.

These aren't just ideas, they come from real experiences we can all relate to.

Heart Truths:
- Healing is something we must work on ourselves. No one else can do it for us.
- Time alone doesn't fix things intentional healing does.
- We can love someone and still need to let them go.
- Personal growth may mean leaving some relationships behind, but it should never mean losing our peace.
- If they really wanted to be in our lives, they would be. Let's stop making excuses for them.

–The Journey Continues

If we were hoping this book would tell us exactly when love will find us,

let's be clear, we don't know. And that's okay.

But here's what we do know:

- We are capable of making smart choices.

- We can heal and grow into the best versions of ourselves.

- We don't have to settle just because we're tired of waiting.

- Our worth isn't tied to our relationship status.

- We are not behind in life. We're exactly where we need to be.

Love isn't something we chase. It's something we prepare for.

Shifting Our Mindset

Our story isn't over. We are still growing, still learning, and still evolving. Every challenge, every lesson, and every difficult decision helped shape us. That person we thought was "the one"? Maybe they were just part of the journey. If they were meant to stay, they would be here. If they're not, we can trust that something better is ahead.

Let's let go of regret. Let's let go of fear. Let's keep moving forward.

New Perspective:

- We avoided a relationship that wasn't right for us.

- We outgrew situations that no longer served us.

- We stopped making excuses and started making better choices.

- We realized that losing them didn't mean losing ourselves.

- We found peace, and that's worth more than any relationship.

Isaiah 61:3 (NLT):
"To all who mourn in Israel, he will give a crown of beauty for ashes, a joyous blessing instead of mourning, festive praise instead of despair. In their righteousness, they will be like great oaks that the Lord has planted for his own glory."

Steps to Apply What We've Learned

1. **Write a Letter to Our Future Selves:** Let's remind ourselves of how much we've grown and where we want to go next.

2. **Set a Personal Standard:** What is one non-negotiable we will stick to in future relationships?

3. **Celebrate Our Growth:** Let's take a moment to recognize how far we've come.

Journal Reflection
- What is the biggest lesson we've learned from this book?

- How has our understanding of love and relationships changed?

- What are we most excited about for the next phase of our lives?

Final Words
This isn't the end. It's just the beginning of our growth, confidence, and transformation. We're not losing in love. We're winning in wisdom.

Now let's go live fully and love wisely.

UP**D**ATE

About the Author

Latia Ashley is an executive producer, entrepreneur, and author with a passion for helping people navigate relationships with wisdom, purpose, and clarity. Her work bridges faith, emotional intelligence, and modern relationship insights, offering a fresh perspective on dating, love, and commitment.

With a background in media and entertainment, Latia brings a unique voice to the conversation one that speaks to both faith-based and secular audiences. She challenges conventional dating norms while staying rooted in biblical principles, making her a trusted guide for those seeking real, lasting love.

When she's not writing, producing, or speaking, Latia is curating spaces for meaningful discussions on love, healing, and self-discovery. She believes that clarity is the key to intentional relationships and lasting covenant.

Follow her journey: @LatiaAshley

Commercial Licensing & Bulk Orders
Interested in using UpDate for church groups, bookstores, coaching programs, or curriculum?
We offer bulk licensing and group study packages!
For bulk orders, podcast interviews, or licensing requests, contact:
Publisher or author
Mailing: P.O Box 1315 Stonecrest Ga 30058

Disclaimer
This book is intended for educational and discussion purposes only. The author does not guarantee specific relationship outcomes, and readers are encouraged to apply biblical principles with wisdom, prayer, and personal discernment.